For Skip—for everything — J. S.

*For Bruce, Brenda, Bobbie, and Booker Henry,
with love* — J. L. P.

Oakville, Alabama, 1920

J. C.'s bare feet
sped along the ground.
He loved playing tag with his friends.
A boy reached out to tag him.
But J. C. dashed away.
The other boys clapped and cheered.
When J. C. Owens ran,
there was no catching him.

J. C. was born in 1913.

His real name was James Cleveland Owens.

He grew up with seven brothers and sisters.

The Owens family lived on a farm.

They worked hard,

raising corn and cotton.

But most of the crops went

to the rich man who owned the land.

The Owens family was poor.

J. C.'s clothes were usually

ragged and thin.

Still, the family always had enough to eat.
And they had each other.
For fun, J. C. and his brothers swam
and fished in a nearby pond.
They liked to hunt in the woods.
On hot summer nights,
they camped by an open fire.

On Sundays, J. C. went to church
with his family.
After church, the men gathered for races.
J. C.'s father was the best runner around.
J. C. thought his father looked
like a rushing train.
He dreamed of running that fast someday.

The Owens family's house was a shack
made of wood and cardboard.
Cold winds blew right through its walls.
Every winter, J. C. became very sick.
His family called it "the devil's cold."
Being sick so much made J. C.
thin and weak.
J. C.'s mother dreamed of a better life
for her children.
It was hard for black families
to get ahead in the South.
Many had moved to cities
in the North.
Maybe the Owenses should, too.

When J. C. was nine, his family
moved to Cleveland, Ohio.
He went to a new school
and made new friends.
People in Cleveland didn't talk the way
J. C. and his family did.
On his first day of school,
J. C.'s teacher asked him his name.
He replied, "J. C.," in his southern accent.
To the teacher, it sounded like "Jesse."
J. C. was too shy to correct her.
From then on, everyone called him Jesse.
Things were better for the Owens family
in Cleveland.
Jesse's father and brothers got jobs
in a steel mill.

At around age 12,
Jesse began working, too.
After school, he pumped gas, shined shoes,
or watered plants in a nursery.

Athlete in Training

When Jesse was 14,
he started junior high school.
His new gym teacher
was Charles Riley.
Coach Riley saw something special in the
new boy with the skinny legs.
He thought Jesse looked like an athlete.

So he asked Jesse to join the track team.

Jesse couldn't wait to tell his parents.

But there was a problem.

The track team trained after school.

That was when Jesse had to work.

So Coach agreed to meet Jesse

before school instead.

Every morning, Jesse got up
an hour early for practice.
The school was empty and quiet.
The only sound was the *crunch crunch*
of Jesse's feet on the track.
He always tried to run the way
Coach taught him.
He held his head high and straight.
He practiced picking up his feet
as soon as he had set them down.
"Run like you're on a red hot stove,"
Coach told him.
Soon he was running with a smooth,
graceful style.
Over the next year,
Jesse's legs became stronger.
He became faster.

One morning, Coach decided to time Jesse
in the 100-yard dash.

Jesse's feet flew toward the finish line.

Coach checked his stopwatch.

That couldn't be right!

Coach found another stopwatch.

Jesse ran again.

The time was the same.

Jesse had run 100 yards in 11 seconds.

That was close to the world record—

the fastest time ever.

Coach Riley had been right.

Jesse Owens was a fine young athlete.

And he was becoming a champion.

One day, a famous runner
visited Jesse's school.
Charley Paddock had won medals
in two Olympic Games.
Jesse was excited to shake his hand.
Right then, he knew that he wanted
to be an Olympic champion, too.
Coach thought Jesse's dream was great.
He told Jesse to think about the future,
not just the next race.
"Train for four years from next Friday,"
Coach said.
Jesse listened, and he kept working hard.

Jesse entered East Tech High School
in 1930.
He kept training with Coach Riley.
Jesse ran 79 races in high school.
He won 75 of them.
He competed in the long jump
and the high jump, too.
Before long, Jesse was doing
more than winning.
He was setting records.
In his senior year,
he set a *world* record in the 220-yard dash.
Crowds loved to watch Jesse run
with his easy, graceful style.
When Jesse was on the field,
people barely noticed anyone else.

Jesse finished high school in 1933.
Many colleges wanted him
to be on their track-and-field team.
Jesse chose Ohio State University.
His new coach was Larry Snyder.
Coach Snyder taught Jesse to run even
faster and jump even farther.
Jesse won event after event
for the Ohio State team.
In May 1935, the team traveled
to Michigan for a championship meet.
Jesse had hurt his back playing football
with friends.

Coach Snyder didn't want Jesse
to compete in the meet.
But Jesse didn't care about the pain.
He knew he could win.

The first event was the 100-yard dash.

For Jesse, the race seemed to be over
as soon as it began.

He won, *and* he tied the world record.

Next was the long jump.

The world record was 26 feet, 2 inches.

Jesse marked that distance with a towel.

He ran toward the take-off board
and leaped into the air.

The towel came closer and closer.
Suddenly it was behind him!
Jesse had shattered the old record
by more than 6 inches.
Minutes later, he broke records in the
220-yard dash and the low hurdles.
In less than an hour, Jesse had set three
records and tied another.

Jesse became famous that day.
Reporters called him
"the world's fastest human."
Everywhere he went,
people wanted to shake his hand.
A few months later,
Jesse had something else to celebrate.
On July 5, 1935,
he married Minnie Ruth Solomon.
Jesse didn't have much time
to enjoy married life.
In the fall, he went back to Ohio State.
Everyone on the track-and-field team
was talking about the Olympic Games.
They would take place the next year, 1936.
Going to the Olympics was all Jesse
could think about.

Jesse tried to study hard in college.
But he had always liked running
better than studying.
He failed one of his classes.
That meant he could not compete
until spring.
Jesse kept training.
But all winter, he had to watch
while his teammates competed.
The Olympic tryouts were coming up.
Would he be ready?

By spring, Jesse could race again.
Once more, he was winning races
and breaking records.
At the Olympic tryouts, it was no surprise
when Jesse finished first in all his events.
His dream was coming true.
He was going to the Olympics.

Olympic Star

Jesse and his American teammates
traveled to Berlin, Germany,
for the Olympic Games.
Adolf Hitler had become
Germany's leader in 1933.

Hitler believed that white Christian
Germans were better than other people.
He especially hated Jews
and people of color.
He believed that white German athletes
would beat everyone else at the Olympics.
That would show the world
his ideas were right.
People all over the world were
horrified by Hitler and his ideas.
They hoped that Jesse and other black
athletes would prove Hitler wrong.

Jesse was not thinking about Hitler.
He said that all he could think about was
"taking home one or two
of those gold medals."
But first he had to solve a problem.
His running shoes were missing.
His coach searched the shops in Berlin
for new shoes.
Just before Jesse's first race,
the coach found two new pairs.
Still, the coach was worried.
Stiff new shoes would hurt Jesse's feet.
That didn't bother Jesse.
"They'll make me jump farther when they
begin to hurt," he said.

Jesse's first event was the 100-meter dash.

A cold rain was falling.

The track was soggy.

But Jesse kept his eyes on the finish line.

Bang! The starter's gun went off.

Jesse sprang into the lead right away.

He crossed the finish nearly 10 feet
ahead of the other runners.
Jesse had won a gold medal.
He had also tied the world record.
He watched proudly as the American flag
was raised for him.

The next day was the long jump.

Each jumper had three tries

to make it to the finals.

Jesse warmed up the way he always did.

He ran down the runway into the pit.

Then he got a surprise.

The judges told him

that this was not allowed.

His warmup would count as one of his tries.

On his second jump, Jesse stepped past

the end of the take-off board.

That was against the rules, too.

He had just one more chance

to make the finals.

Jesse was afraid.

Suddenly, Jesse felt a hand on his shoulder.

It was Lutz Long, a German long jumper.

Lutz was Jesse's toughest rival.

What could he have to say to Jesse?

Lutz knew Jesse was scared.

He told Jesse not to worry.

Jesse's jumps were long enough, he said.

The important thing was

to not make another mistake.

Lutz told Jesse to place a mark a few inches

behind the take-off board.

Jump from there, he said.

Then Jesse would be sure

he would not overstep again.

Jesse smiled.

It was a great idea!

He relaxed, and then he made his jump.

This time it was good.

It was time for the long jump finals.

At first, Jesse was ahead.

Then Lutz jumped just as far as he had.

On his third and final jump,

Jesse burst off the take-off board.

One reporter said he looked like he was
jumping "clear out of Germany."
When he landed, he had won the gold.
Lutz Long won the silver medal.
He rushed to Jesse's side
and shook his hand.
The two athletes left the field arm in arm.

Jesse also won gold medals
in the 200-meter dash
and the 400-meter relay.
He had set four Olympic records.
Hitler was disappointed.
But the German crowds loved Jesse.
They chanted his name from the stands.
His picture was in newspapers
all over the world.
Jesse had made his dream come true.
He was an Olympic champion.
And he was an American hero.

Afterword

By the time Jesse returned from the Olympics, he and his wife, Ruth, had already had the first of their three daughters. Jesse needed to earn a living, and he tried lots of jobs. He was a bandleader, public speaker, and owner of a basketball team, and he started a dry-cleaning business. He was also paid to run exhibition races at events such as baseball games.

Throughout his life, Jesse was in demand as a public speaker. People liked his strong voice and his stories. Jesse's message was positive and inspiring—people in the United States, regardless of their color or background, could achieve their dreams through hard work and determination.

One of Jesse's favorite subjects was how Lutz Long helped him during the long jump trials at the 1936 Olympics. Many people have questioned the truth of this story, since no one actually saw Jesse and Lutz talking together that day. But Jesse always stuck to his story. He called his friendship with Lutz his "greatest Olympic prize."

As he grew older, Jesse continued to travel all over the world, giving speeches, presenting awards, and appearing at athletic events. He also wrote four books about his life and his beliefs. In 1980, Jesse Owens died at age 66. He will always be remembered for his dedication and determination and for his amazing Olympic achievements.

Important Dates

1913—James Cleveland Owens was born in Oakville, Alabama, on September 12.

1922—Moved to Cleveland, Ohio, with his family

1927—Entered Fairmount Junior High School; met Coach Charles Riley

1930—Entered East Technical High School

1933—Won three events at the National Interscholastic Championship in Chicago, Illinois; entered Ohio State University

1935—Broke three world records and tied another at the Big Ten Track and Field Championships in Michigan; married Minnie Ruth Solomon

1936—Won four gold medals at the Olympic Games in Berlin, Germany

1950—Named Outstanding Track Athlete of the Half Century by the Associated Press

1955—Began traveling widely as goodwill ambassador for the U.S. State Department

1973—Appointed to the Board of Directors of the United States Olympic Committee

1974—Elected to the Track and Field Hall of Fame

1976—Awarded the Medal of Freedom by President Gerald Ford

1979—Awarded the Living Legends Award by President Jimmy Carter

1980—Died of cancer in Tucson, Arizona, on March 31